TJ's Book

David

I cotn your
book bich

Do not

take

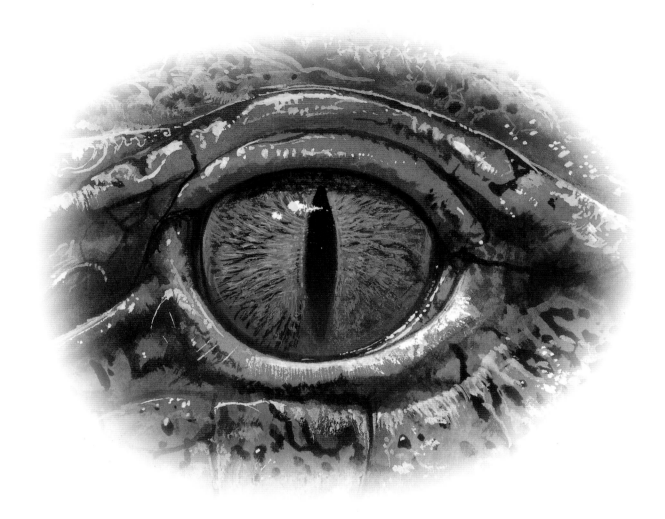

LIFE-SIZE REPTILES

WRITTEN BY
HANNAH WILSON

Sterling Publishing Co., Inc.
New York

First published in the UK in 2007 by Pavilion Children's Books,
an imprint of Anova Books plc,
151 Freston Road, London, W10 6TH, UK.

Library of Congress Cataloging-in-Publication Date Available

10 9 8 7 6 5 4 3 2

Published in 2007 by Sterling Publishing Co., Inc.
387 Park Avenue South, New York, NY 10016

Distributed in Canada by Sterling Publishing
c/o Canadian Manda Group, 165 Dufferin Street
Toronto, Ontario, Canada M6K 3H6

Sterling ISBN-13: 978-1-4027-5299-5
    ISBN-10: 1-4027-5299-7

For information about custom editions,
special sales, premium and corporate
purchases, please contact Sterling Special
Sales Department at 800-805-5489 or
specialsales@sterlingpub.com.

Contents

Staying alive

Most reptiles run away when they are under attack, but for lumbering tortoises that is not an option. Instead, they retreat into their armored shells. Other reptiles stay out of sight by being camouflaged. A chameleon can even change its color to match its surroundings! Other reptiles do not need to hide away. Coral snakes, for example, are brightly colored. This warns attackers that the snake's bite contains a deadly venom.

LIFE-SIZE

This skink is using a drastic defense tactic. The raccoon bites the bright blue tail of its prey instead of the head. The tail breaks off and continues to wriggle while the skink dashes to safety. The lizard soon grows a new tail.

Killing tactics

Most reptiles are hunters. Many kill a wide range of prey, but some are specialists. It's pretty clear what's on the menu for the ratsnake or the egg-eating snake. Reptiles catch their prey with their teeth, claws, or even a sticky tongue. Turtles slice up prey with sharp, beak-like jaws, while crocodiles drown antelopes by spinning them around underwater.

The reticulated python is a constrictor, it crushes its prey to death with its coils. This python is the world's longest snake, growing to 49 feet (15 meters), that's the length of a city bus!

Sensory skills

Reptiles have poor hearing. Some don't even have any ear openings at all. The forked tongues of snakes and some lizards are not very good at tasting either. Strangely, they are used for smelling instead. The tips of the tongue pick up scent particles in the air. The tips then slide into slots in the roof the mouth, so the reptile can detect the smells.

Reptiles have some other unusual sensory skills. Some snakes detect the heat given off by prey, using dips, or "pits", on their faces. And many lizards have a light-sensitive "third eye" inside the top of their skulls.

LIFE-SIZE

LIFE-SIZE

The long-nosed whipsnake has horizontal pupils so it can see to the front and to the side at the same time. To focus on its prey, it looks down grooves on its long snout, in the same way an archer looks along the length of an arrow to aim at a target.

The eyes of a chameleon can move independently and point in two different directions at the same time. This allows the lizard to scan its surroundings for food.

Eggs and babies

Most reptiles lay eggs, carefully hiding them in nests, but some snakes, such as rattlesnakes, and many lizards give birth to their young. Infant reptiles look like miniature adults, although their coloring is often different. Pythons are among the best reptile parents, a female will coil herself around the eggs. Her body keeps them warm until the young hatch.

LIFE-SIZE

A baby hawksbill turtle pushes its way out of its egg. Like bird eggs, reptile eggs have yolks, which nourish the young as they grow inside.

WHAT IS A REPTILE?

Scaly, spiky, horned, clawed or venomous, many reptiles are formidable creatures. Most belong to a group called the squamates, which includes lizards and snakes. Turtles and tortoises make up the second-largest group, while crocodiles and alligators account for less than one percent of all reptiles.

Reptiles long ago

Reptiles began to evolve about 340 million years ago from four-legged creatures that laid soft eggs in water. Reptilian eggs developed waterproof shells so they could be laid on dry land. The reptiles grew tough scaly skin and stronger skeletons as they adapted to a land-based life. And they grew larger. Much larger.

Some reptiles have changed little in millions of years. Proganochelys lived more than 200 million years ago but looked very much like a modern turtle.

Some prehistoric reptiles, like this pterosaur, could fly.

Many dinosaurs, like Plateosaurus, walked on their hind legs.

Saurosuchus, one of the first reptiles, was not a dinosaur but a relative of crocodiles.

About 200 million years ago, Earth was ruled by giant reptiles, dinosaurs. But the dinosaurs came to a dramatic end 65 million years ago when an asteroid (space rock) hit Earth. This produced an immense dust cloud that darkened the skies for years. Today's reptiles, like crocodiles and snakes, made it through the devastation. But the changes killed the dinosaurs. Only their descendants, birds, survive.

Sunbathing

Reptiles have no fur or feathers to keep them warm and cannot control their body temperature from the inside. Instead, they gain or lose heat from their surroundings, they are warmed by the sun or cooled by water. This is called "ectothermy". Many reptiles have to bask in the morning sun to warm up before beginning to hunt.

powerful tail used for swimming

bony plates strengthen scales

Reptiles do not sweat through their tough skins, so alligators pant with their mouths open to cool down.

long claws

The body of this alligator is typical of many reptiles. It is low-lying, with short legs sticking out the side.

The teeth grow throughout the reptile's life.

Scaly skin

Reptilian scales are made of keratin, the same substance in your hair and fingernails. Scales make the skin waterproof. They can be thickened to form armored plates or shells. Scales do not grow, so a reptile sheds its skin when it becomes too small for it.

Snakes, such as this garter snake, can shed their skin all at once, but lizards shed skin in pieces because their legs get in the way.

LIFE-SIZE

LIZARDS

With more than 3,000 species, lizards can be as small as ladybugs or as large as alligators. Spotty, striped, smooth, or spiky, they live in deserts, jungles, and even the ocean. And some don't even have legs, if you see a slow worm in your garden, remember it's not a worm at all, nor a snake, it's a lizard!

Sticky fingers

Geckos are small lizards with a special talent, climbing. They can scale vertical walls, even windows, and they can scuttle upside down across ceilings. Many of them have have rounded pads at the tips of each toe. These pads spread out so the toes "stick" to surfaces.

Many geckos also make sounds. The tokay, the largest of all geckos, is named after its "to-kay" bark.

The tokay gecko lives in the jungles of southeast Asia. It ventures into the "concrete jungle" of cities, too. At night, it emerges from cracks in walls to hunt insects.

LIFE-SIZE

The bottom of each toe pad is covered in small overlapping scales. Each scale has thousands of tiny hair-like projections that stick to surfaces.

Tokay gecko

Tiny lizards

At only 16 millimeters long, the dwarf gecko is not just the smallest lizard, it is the smallest of all reptiles, birds, and mammals. Seen here at three times its actual size, the geckos live among the leaves on the forest floors of some Caribbean islands. Their habitat is under threat from deforestation, and their lives are not made easier by their size. Their tiny bodies cannot store much water, and the geckos risk drying out. And when you're not much bigger than an ant, many insects are predators rather than prey.

Nile monitor

Monitors can rear up on their hind legs, supported by their tail. They stand up to have a look around or to fight a rival.

Lizard kings

The largest lizards of all are the monitor lizards. And reaching 6.5 feet (2 meters) in length, the Nile monitor certainly measures up. This impressive creature is the largest African lizard. It is a strong swimmer and is never far from water. Its nostrils are positioned high on its snout so that it can breathe when swimming. The monitor uses sharp claws to kill the fish, crabs, and frogs in the water. It even braves attacks from mother crocs to steal eggs from their nests!

Tongues on target

The chameleon takes its time when hunting for a tasty insect. Clinging to a branch with its toes and tail, only its protruding eyes move, swiveling in different directions in search of a hopping cricket or a buzzing fly. Once the prey has been targeted, the chameleon shoots out its tongue, which can be longer than its body. The insect is ensnared by the tongue's sticky tip.

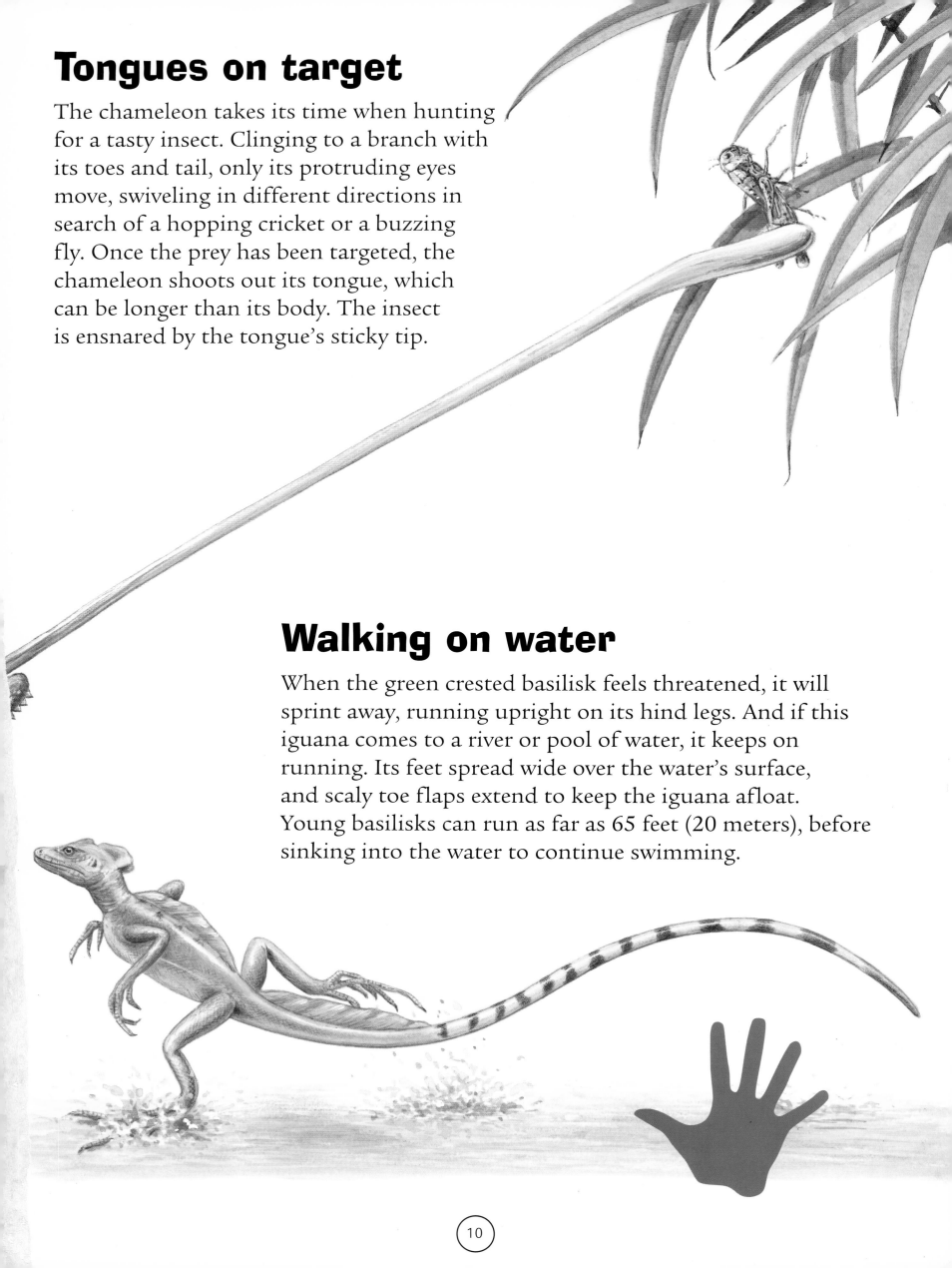

Walking on water

When the green crested basilisk feels threatened, it will sprint away, running upright on its hind legs. And if this iguana comes to a river or pool of water, it keeps on running. Its feet spread wide over the water's surface, and scaly toe flaps extend to keep the iguana afloat. Young basilisks can run as far as 65 feet (20 meters), before sinking into the water to continue swimming.

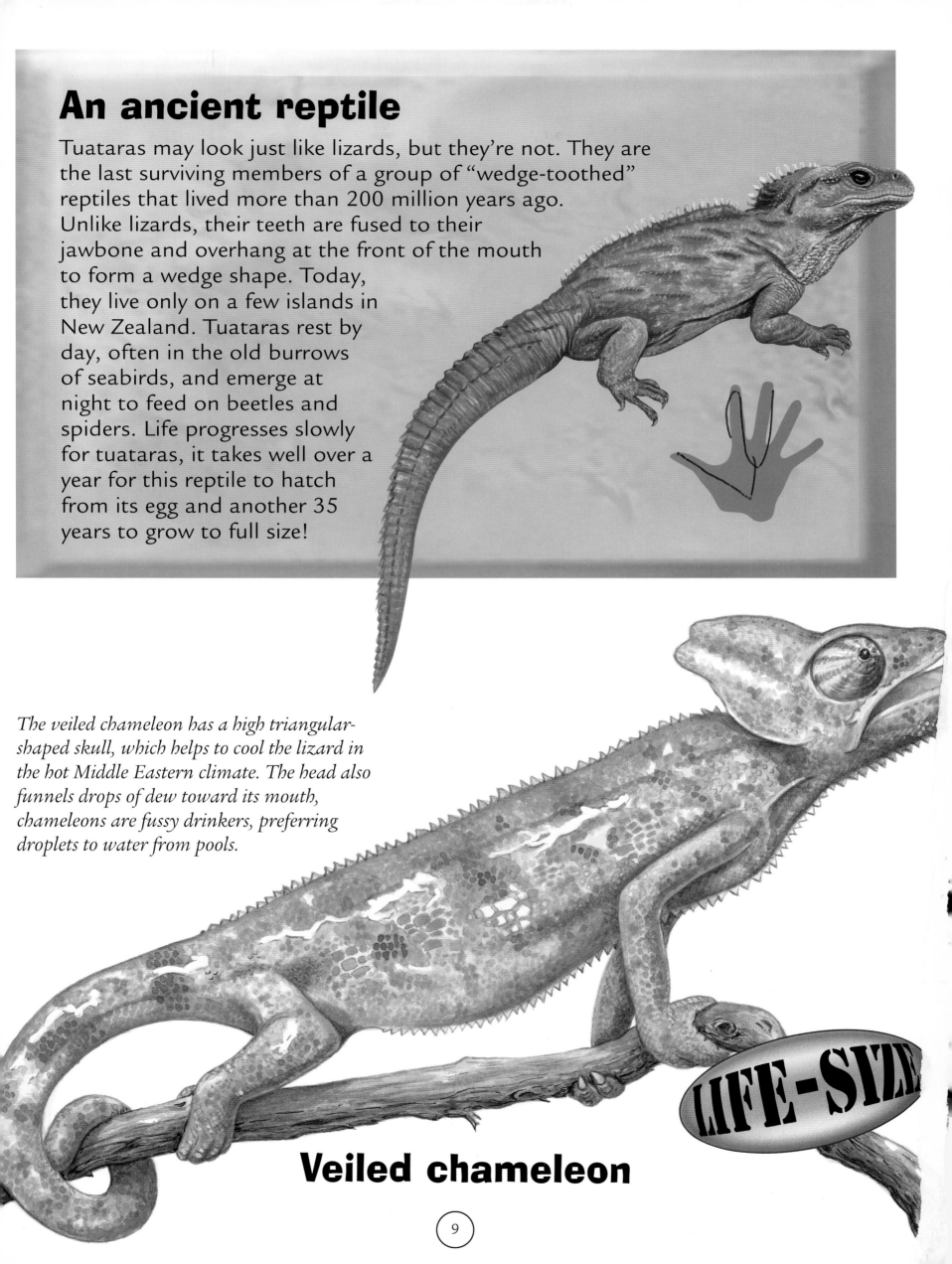

An ancient reptile

Tuataras may look just like lizards, but they're not. They are the last surviving members of a group of "wedge-toothed" reptiles that lived more than 200 million years ago. Unlike lizards, their teeth are fused to their jawbone and overhang at the front of the mouth to form a wedge shape. Today, they live only on a few islands in New Zealand. Tuataras rest by day, often in the old burrows of seabirds, and emerge at night to feed on beetles and spiders. Life progresses slowly for tuataras, it takes well over a year for this reptile to hatch from its egg and another 35 years to grow to full size!

The veiled chameleon has a high triangular-shaped skull, which helps to cool the lizard in the hot Middle Eastern climate. The head also funnels drops of dew toward its mouth, chameleons are fussy drinkers, preferring droplets to water from pools.

LIFE-SIZE

Veiled chameleon

A lizard of the ocean

The marine iguana of the Galápagos Islands in the Pacific Ocean is the only lizard truly adapted to an ocean life. With webbed feet and a powerful tail that acts like a rudder, this creature can swim beneath the waves, grazing on the plants and algae that cling to the rocky seabed. The lizards generally feed in shallow water and are under the water for about ten minutes at a time. Large iguanas can dive to a depth of 49 feet (15 meters) and stay underwater for more than an hour when they need to.

LIFE-SIZE

Marine iguana

Color changes

When marine iguanas emerge from the cold ocean, their wet bodies are black. This helps them to absorb heat as they dry out in the sun on the rocky shoreline. They become paler after sunbathing. All marine iguanas have white-streaked faces, this is caused by the sea salt that they continually spray from their noses!

Like many iguanas, this lizard has a spiky crest along its back. Males are larger than the females and grow to 4.3 feet (1.3 meters). When the males are ready to mate, their bodies develop colorful streaks.

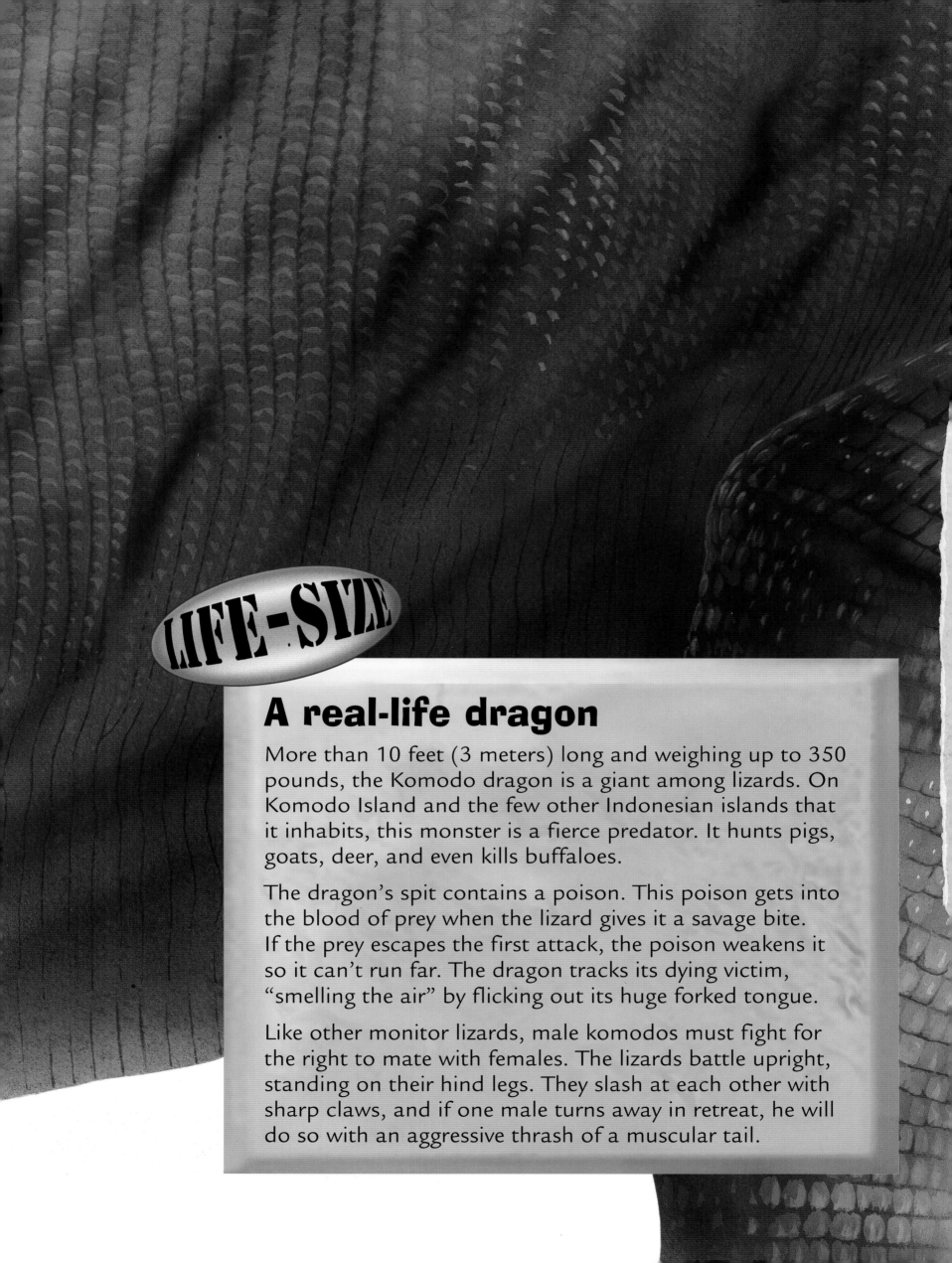

LIFE-SIZE

A real-life dragon

More than 10 feet (3 meters) long and weighing up to 350 pounds, the Komodo dragon is a giant among lizards. On Komodo Island and the few other Indonesian islands that it inhabits, this monster is a fierce predator. It hunts pigs, goats, deer, and even kills buffaloes.

The dragon's spit contains a poison. This poison gets into the blood of prey when the lizard gives it a savage bite. If the prey escapes the first attack, the poison weakens it so it can't run far. The dragon tracks its dying victim, "smelling the air" by flicking out its huge forked tongue.

Like other monitor lizards, male komodos must fight for the right to mate with females. The lizards battle upright, standing on their hind legs. They slash at each other with sharp claws, and if one male turns away in retreat, he will do so with an aggressive thrash of a muscular tail.

Trunks and treetops

Many lizards are adapted to living among the trees of jungles and forests. They have "prehensile" tails that wrap around branches and feet built for gripping tree trunks. But the flying dragon doesn't bother with climbing for long jungle trips, it can glide between the treetops by extending flaps of skin that act like wings. The Australian frilled lizard also has flaps, but not for flying. In an impressively fierce display designed to scare off any hungry python, it opens a leathery frill around its neck, rocks backward and forward and hisses menacingly.

The bright pink gaping mouth and the orange frill – up to 1 foot (30 centimeters) wide, would startle any predator that moments before was facing a small brown lizard!

Frilled lizard

LIFE-SIZE

Desert dwellers

Lizards, like all reptiles, need to sunbathe to keep themselves warm, so life in hot, sunny deserts suits them well. Once they have reached their desired body temperature, the desert lizards climb trees in search of a cool breeze, seek shade in a rocky crevice, or simply lift their bodies as far above the hot sand as possible. Desert lizards don't drink. A diet of insects, often several thousand a day, provides the lizards with all the water they need.

LIFE-SIZE

Gila monster

The gila monster copes with the heat by emerging mainly at night. Covered with bead-like scales, it kills prey, such as rats or frogs, with a poisonous bite. It is one of only two species of lizard that are venomous.

The spines of the thorny devil help camouflage it among the stones of the Australian desert. And if the camouflage fails, predators are put off by such a spiky snack! Grooves between the spikes channel drops of moisture to the mouth, so the lizard does not waste any water.

Thorny devil

LIFE-SIZE

Komodo dragon

SNAKES

These strange fanged creatures, often with forked tongues, slit-like eyes and vivid colors, are unhindered by their lack of limbs. Snakes are masterful movers, silently slithering, climbing, burrowing, and even swimming through the world's warm regions.

LIFE-SIZE

Emerald tree boa

Snakes come in all shapes and sizes. Ground snakes are often short, heavy, and wide, whereas tree snakes, like this emerald tree boa, have long, slender bodies. Snakes' tails are more flexible than their bodies because they lack ribs. The tails of tree boas are prehensile, which means that they can grip onto branches.

Swimming snakes

The pelagic sea snake is one of the most venomous snakes of all, and its bright yellow belly warns sharks to keep away as it swims through the Pacific and Indian Oceans. This snake is perfectly adapted for an ocean life. Its tail is shaped like a paddle and it cannot move easily on land. Like marine iguanas, the snake cleans salt from its body, using glands under its tongue. The snake can remain underwater for more than three hours before returning to the surface to breathe. Often thousands of sea snakes drift together in a writhing mass of black and yellow scales.

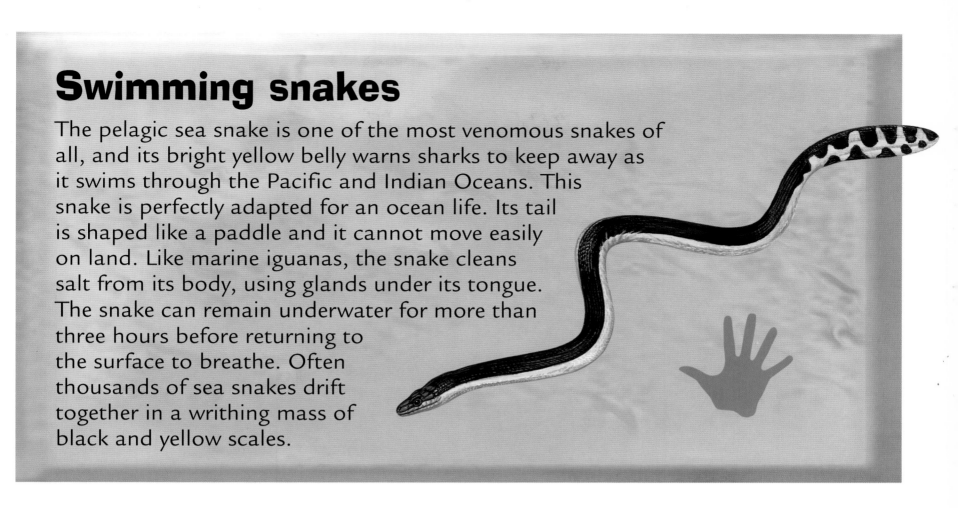

Big mouths

Imagine trying to swallow something three times the size of your head. That is exactly what an egg-eating snake can do. Snakes can't chew food or rip it apart with claws so they must swallow it whole. Flexible jaws open wide, and elastic skin stretches over the egg, allowing it to pass through the throat into the stomach without ripping the snake apart. Anacondas and pythons perform the same trick but on a much larger scale, swallowing antelopes or even caimans whole. Snakes that eat such huge meals can go for weeks or months without eating again.

Blindsnake

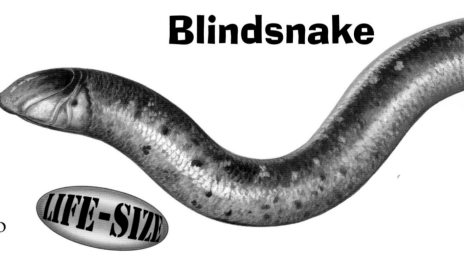

The blindsnake cannot see at all. In fact, its skin has grown over its eyes completely. The snake has a smooth scale on its face that acts like a spade. Unlike other snakes, the blindsnake can't open its mouth wide, but this isn't a problem when tiny termites are on the menu.

Egg-eating snake

Snakes great and small

There are 2,800 species of snake. They live across the world, from the chilly forests of Canada to the scorching deserts of Australia.

The largest snake in the world is the mighty green anaconda, which lives in the swamps and jungles of South America. Females are bigger than males and can grow to 33feet (10 meters) and weigh a quarter of ton! An anaconda does not bite its prey to death. Instead, the snake crushes its victim with its immense coils, squeezing so tightly that the prey cannot breathe. Large anacondas even kill other hunters such as caimans and jaguars. A hungry anaconda will also eat you if given the chance!

The smallest snake in the world is the Lesser-Antillean threadsnake, which could probably slither through a pencil if the lead was removed. This snake lives underground and is sometimes called the "worm snake".

Anacondas have many small, pointed teeth that hook onto prey as it is slowly swallowed. Prey might still be alive even as it is engulfed by the snake. But it cannot escape the snake's firm bite.

A sticky snout

The odd-looking leafnose vinesnake, from the island of Madagascar in the Indian Ocean, is a master of disguise. Its rough brown scales help the long, slender snake to resemble a twig. The female leafnose has another trick up its sleeve, or rather on its snout, a projection that looks just like a fir cone!

Warning rattle

The warning buzz of a rattlesnake's tail is a familiar sound in the deserts and scrubland of North America. The rattle is formed from scaly segments that do not fall off when the snake sheds its skin. The segments collect around the tip of the tail and rattle together when the snake shakes them. The rattle gets larger, and louder, every time this venomous viper sheds its skin.

Pits on the snake's face detect the body heat of prey.

The short rattle shows that this is a young snake.

Snakes might look as if they have no eyelids, but in fact both upper and lower sets are fused (joined together) to protect the eyes. The lids are made of transparent skin so the snakes can see through them.

LIFE-SIZE

Loose sand is a slippery surface, and desert snakes cannot push against it to move forward. Instead, many of them move with a motion known as sidewinding. The snakes lift sections of their bodies across the sand in a diagonal direction. The master of this movement is the sidewinder (left), a rattlesnake from North America.

④

③ Snakes can move by bunching their curved bodies together like an accordian and then stretching out again, so their bodies end up further forward. Tree snakes do this to reach across gaps between branches. Burrowing snakes move in a similar way, pushing their bodies against the walls of a tunnel.

The flying snakes of Southeast Asia cannot actually fly. Instead, they glide through the air and can travel 330 feet (100 meters) at a time as they leap from tree to tree. These snakes have flat bodies, and they spread their ribs to make a wing-like surface that catches the air.

Slither and slide

A snake's body is packed full of muscles and that makes it very strong yet flexible at the same time. Many snakes can even tie themselves in knots! Not having any legs does not stop snakes from getting around. They can twist, thrust and pull their bodies over or under ground, through trees, across deserts and even glide through the air. Snakes move in a number of ways, using different parts of their bodies to push themselves along.

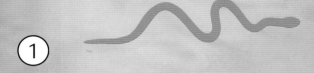

①

Most snakes move by wriggling their bodies from side to side. This is called lateral undulation. Muscles contract on just one side of each section of the snake, and this creates S-shaped curves that move down the body like a wave. The curved body pushes against bumps on the ground to force the snake forward.

②

Heavy snakes like pythons move in a straight line, and it is often difficult to see how they do it. Sections of the body are lifted slightly off the ground. The scales left touching the ground hook onto the rough surface so the snake can heave itself along. This type of movement is slow but silent, and snakes use it when stalking prey.

Green anaconda

King of the snakes

If you annoy a king cobra, you'll probably regret it. The longest venomous snake in the world, reaching more than 16 feet (5 meters) in length, can rear up and look you straight in the eye. And if it gets really annoyed, it will flatten its upper ribs, creating a scaly hood, and hiss loudly. If that warning does not scare you away, the snake will strike, delivering a bite at incredible speed. The king cobra's venom is so powerful that it can kill an elephant in three hours. However, this Indian snake is more interested in catching its next meal, usually another snake!

LIFE-SIZE

Venomous fangs

Snakes inject venom into their prey to paralyze or kill it and make it easier to swallow. Venom is produced by glands in the jaw. When the snake bites, a muscle pumps the venom through a tube, or duct, toward the fangs. The venom then flows through hollows in the fangs or grooves on the outside. Spitting cobras spray clouds of venom from openings at the front of their fangs in an attempt to blind their prey. The most poisonous snake is the Australian taipan. The venom in a single bite could kill 100 people.

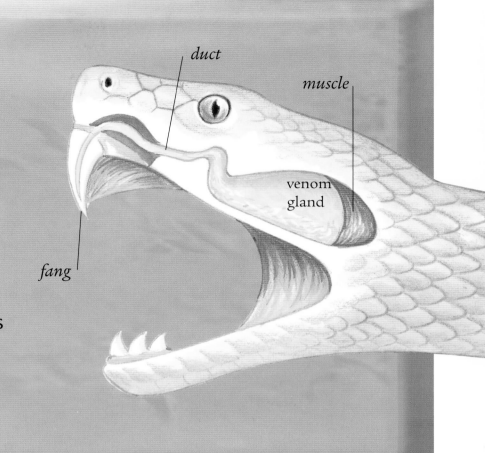

duct

muscle

venom gland

fang

Unlike many other snakes, the female king cobra builds a sophisticated nest. She piles up dead leaves and soil and creates a hollow for up to 50 eggs. Just before the eggs hatch, the cobra instinctively leaves the nest to prevent herself from eating her own offspring.

Saltwater crocodile

LIFE-SIZE

Ruler of the reptiles

The mightiest reptile on Earth, up to 26 feet (8 meters) in length and weighing more than a ton, is the ferocious saltwater crocodile. This beast is one of the animal kingdom's most dangerous predators and its favorite tactic is ambush. It lies in wait in the shallows of a river or swamp, only its eyes and nostrils are exposed above the water. If a buffalo comes for a drink, the croc will rush from the water and deliver a devastating bite. Its mighty jaws can snap antelope legs like twigs and crush turtle shells like crackers. The beast drags its prey back into the water and drowns it, often by spinning its victims underwater so they cannot struggle free.

CROCODILES

The largest reptiles on Earth are the fearsome crocodilians. These include the crocodiles, alligators, caimans and the strange-snouted gharial. With their long, toothy jaws, powerful tails, and tough armor plates, these carnivores are the rulers of their watery habitats.

The eyes, nostrils, and ears of this Cuban crocodile are at the top of the head so that they sit above the water. Unlike most reptiles, crocs have a third transparent eyelid that moves horizontally across the eye to protect it when the croc is underwater.

Ancient hunters

Crocodilians have survived unchanged since before the dinosaurs roamed the Earth. That is because crocs are perfect underwater killing machines. They paddle with webbed hind feet and use their powerful tail as a rudder. They can even eat fish or other prey underwater by closing a flap of skin in their throats to stop water from entering their lungs. But crocs don't just hunt in the water, the Cuban crocodile can leap completely out of a river to snatch a lizard from an overhanging branch.

Little and large

This baby American alligator may be small, but it still has sharp teeth and a strong jaw that can deliver a nasty bite. The alligator takes about ten years to grow to full adult size. By then the alligator will have lost its distinctive yellow bands because its skin will be coated with dark algae from its watery habitat. And it will reach 16 feet (5 meters) in length, that's pretty big for an alligator, which along with their relatives, the caimans, tend to be smaller than crocodiles.

LIFE-SIZE

Happy families

The Chinese alligator is very similar to the American alligator but is smaller, reaching no more than 6.5 feet (2 meters) long. Like all crocodilians, it is a good parent. The mother alligator is alerted to her newborns by their chorus of squeaks. She will dig the babies out of the muddy nest and carry them gently in her mouth to a safe place.

If the young alligators are struggling to get out of their shells, their mother will gently roll the eggs into her mouth to help crack them open.

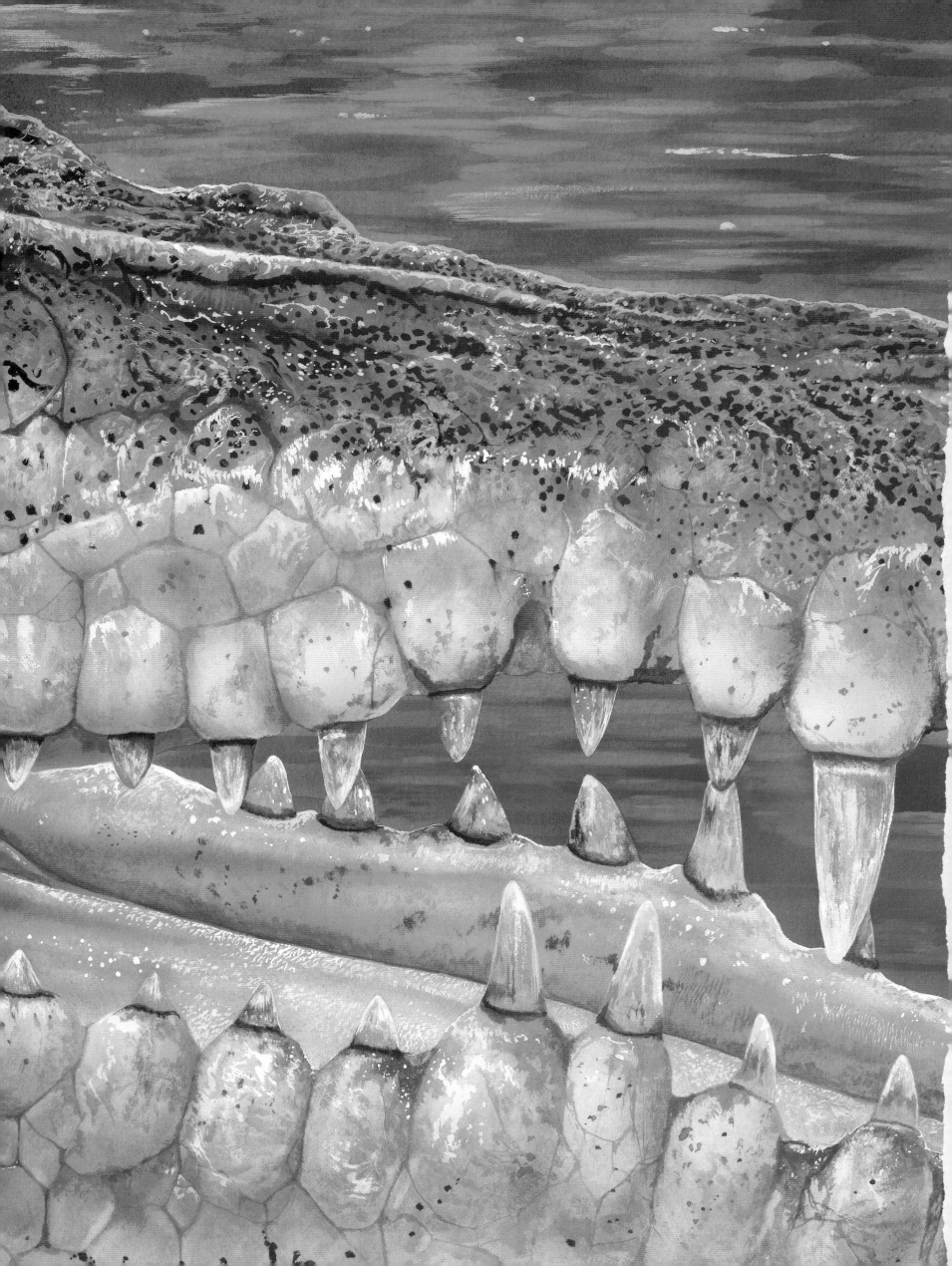

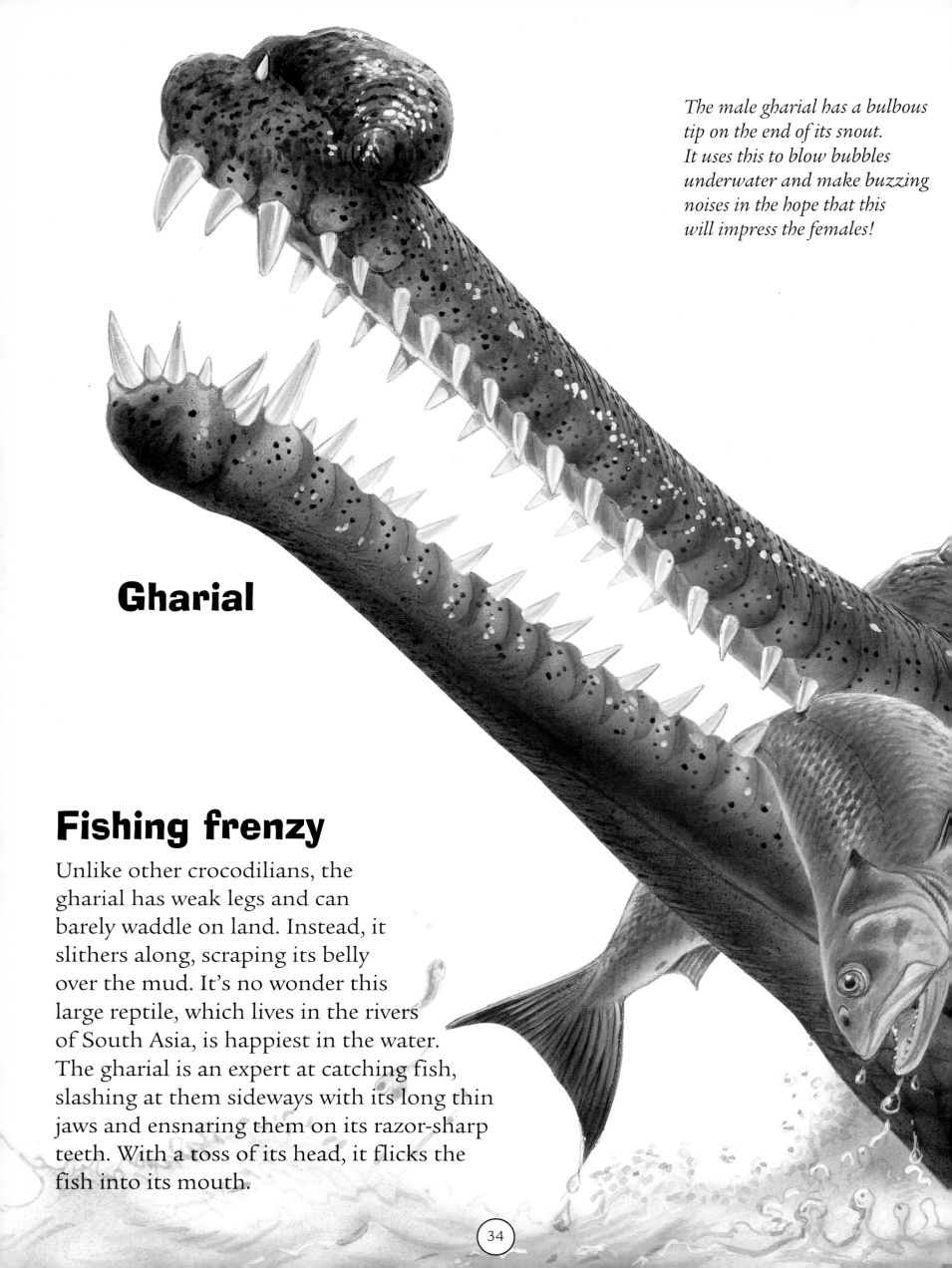

Gharial

The male gharial has a bulbous tip on the end of its snout. It uses this to blow bubbles underwater and make buzzing noises in the hope that this will impress the females!

Fishing frenzy

Unlike other crocodilians, the gharial has weak legs and can barely waddle on land. Instead, it slithers along, scraping its belly over the mud. It's no wonder this large reptile, which lives in the rivers of South Asia, is happiest in the water. The gharial is an expert at catching fish, slashing at them sideways with its long thin jaws and ensnaring them on its razor-sharp teeth. With a toss of its head, it flicks the fish into its mouth.

Toothy grins

The differences between the crocodilians can be observed by looking at their heads, and in particular their teeth. All crocodilians have at least 60 teeth and these are replaced many times throughout their life, one croc can get through as many as 3,000 teeth!

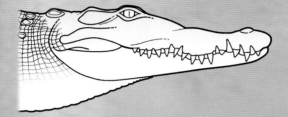

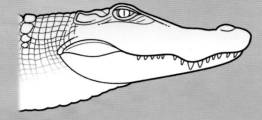

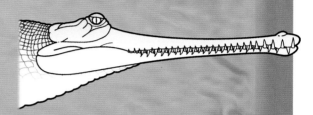

Crocodiles have long, V-shaped snouts. Both sets of teeth are exposed when their mouths are shut, giving crocs a toothy grin.

Alligators have shorter, rounded snouts. The upper jaw is wider than the lower one and covers the bottom teeth.

Gharials have very long and slender snouts with evenly spaced teeth that interconnect like a zipper.

Gentle giant

This enormous scaly creature can weigh as much as an adult lion and live for 150 years. It lives its long, slow life on the Galápagos Islands in the Pacific Ocean, enjoying a morning sunbathe, followed by a search for a leafy meal and a snooze in a muddy hollow. The shape of a Galápagos tortoise shell depends on the habitat of the island where it lives. Tortoises that live on islands with low-lying vegetation have large, domed shells that prevent them from raising their heads upward. On other islands, tortoises have saddleback shells with a cut-out section behind the neck that allows them to reach up to munch on the leaves of taller plants.

LIFE-SIZE

TORTOISES AND TURTLES

Lumbering slowly over ground or swimming gracefully underwater, these largely sluggish reptiles are not the greatest hunters, often preferring to graze on vegetation on the forest or ocean floor. Tortoises and turtles may lack attack skills, but, with their armored shells, they're pretty good at defense.

Armored crawlers

Unlike turtles, which need smooth, flattened shells to slip through water easily, most tortoises have shells that are high and bumpy, a shape designed to put off any predator. The pancake tortoise uses a different defense tactic, its shell is flat. This allows it to fit into narrow crevices in its rocky African habitat.

LIFE-SIZE

Indian star tortoise

A tortoise's shell is made up of plates, or scutes, that sit on a domed layer of bone, that is part of the skeleton. The scutes contain pigments that give tortoises their patterned shells. The number of rings on a scute can indicate a tortoise's age, a bit like the rings inside a tree trunk.

Ocean voyager

The leatherback is the largest turtle in the world, and one of the heaviest reptiles. It reaches about 8 feet (2.5 meters) in both length and width (with its flippers extended). It can weigh up to 1,750 pounds, the same as five komodo dragons. This enormous creature swims thousands of miles every year in search of jellyfish, which it catches with its hooked beak. The turtle takes its name from its supple leathery shell, which is lighter than the hard shells of other marine turtles.

Like all marine turtles, the leatherback has flippers (although uniquely, theirs are clawless). It doesn't need legs for walking like most freshwater turtles. Male leatherbacks never come on land and females spend just two hours ashore every few years, when they haul themselves onto a beach to lay eggs.

**Giant
tortoise**

Snorkeling snouts

Like all swimming reptiles, turtles must return to the surface of the water to breathe. The matamata of the Amazon, however, avoids this inconvenience by snorkeling. This weird-looking river turtle has a long tube-shaped snout with nostrils on the end. It pokes the snout above the water to take a breath. A river turtle from Australia goes to even further extremes to avoid surfacing, it breathes through its bottom! By pumping water into its backside, it can extract enough oxygen to stay underwater for three days.

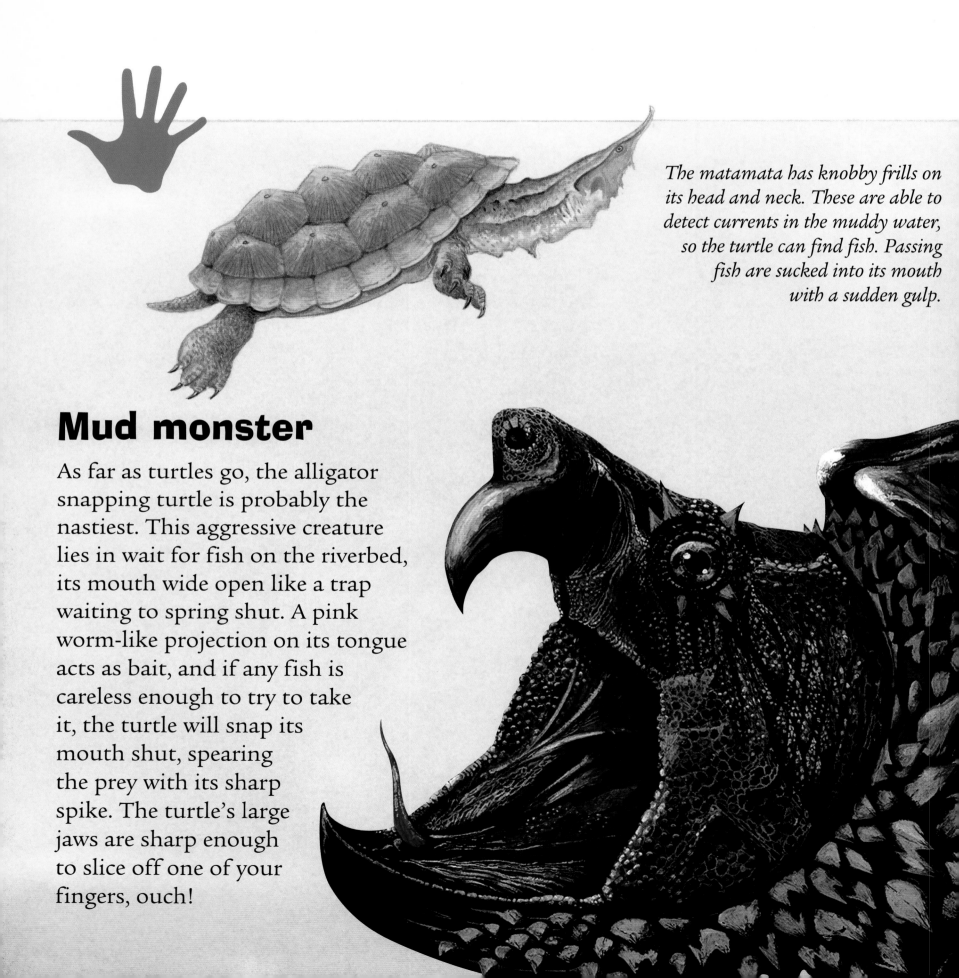

The matamata has knobby frills on its head and neck. These are able to detect currents in the muddy water, so the turtle can find fish. Passing fish are sucked into its mouth with a sudden gulp.

Mud monster

As far as turtles go, the alligator snapping turtle is probably the nastiest. This aggressive creature lies in wait for fish on the riverbed, its mouth wide open like a trap waiting to spring shut. A pink worm-like projection on its tongue acts as bait, and if any fish is careless enough to try to take it, the turtle will snap its mouth shut, spearing the prey with its sharp spike. The turtle's large jaws are sharp enough to slice off one of your fingers, ouch!

Taking cover

To take full advantage of their protective shells, most turtles and tortoises hide their heads inside them when danger is near. Different species take cover in different ways, and many can also withdraw their legs into their shells, too. However, a few turtles, such as the leatherback, cannot hide their heads at all.

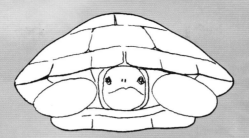

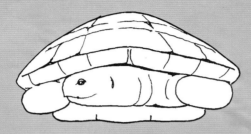

Tortoises and straight-necked turtles lower their heads and fold their necks into an S-shape under their spines. The head appears to move backward into the shell in a straight line.

Side-necked turtles have longer necks than the straight-necked species. They bend them to one side, hiding them under the lip of their shells.

The alligator snapping turtle is the largest river turtle in North America. It grows up to 31 inches (80 centimeters) in length.

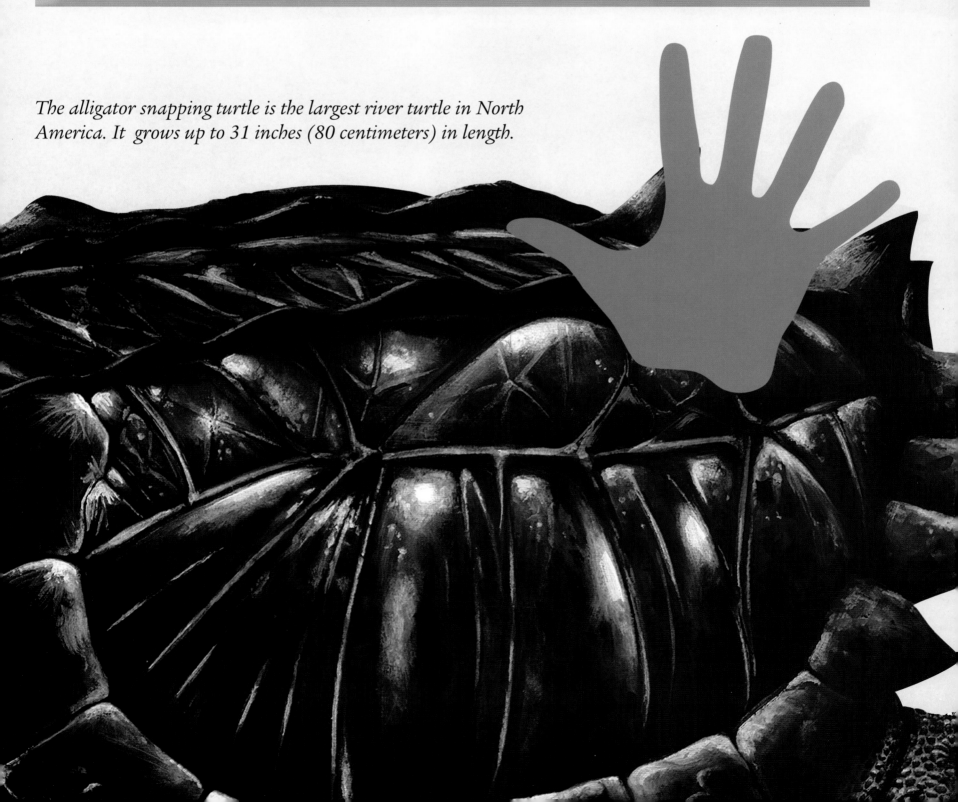

REPTILES AT RISK

The biggest threat to reptiles is humankind. Despite many protection laws, we still hunt them for food and for their skins, we capture them to sell as pets, and we destroy their habitats. If we don't stop, many of the species you have just read about, and more, will become extinct.

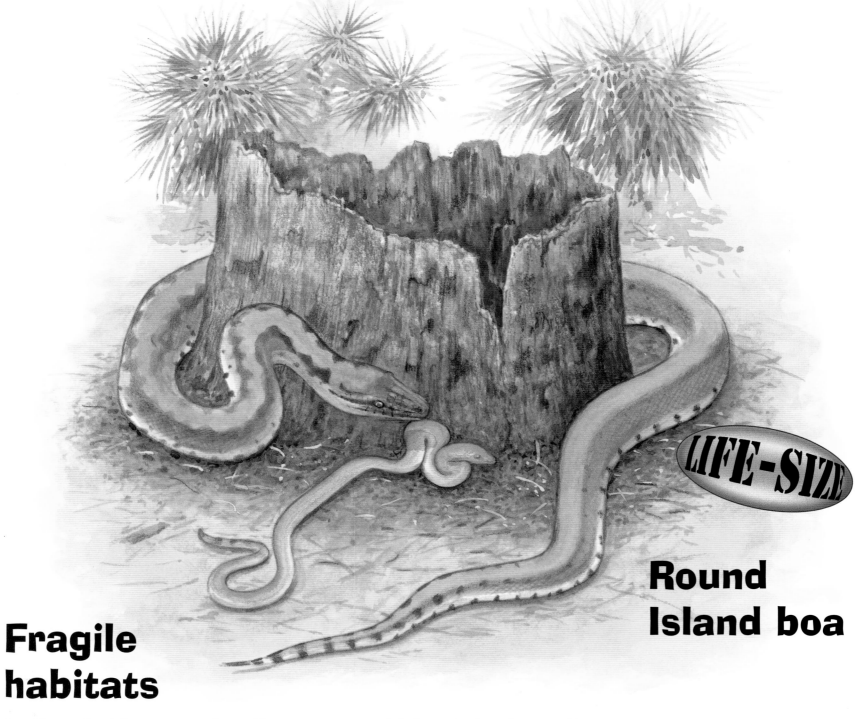

LIFE-SIZE

Round Island boa

Fragile habitats

Keel-scaled boas used to live on several islands in the Indian Ocean. They now survive on just one, tiny Round Island near Mauritius. The snakes died out elsewhere when rats were introduced to the islands. The boas were bred in zoos to boost their numbers, and their palm-forest habitat is protected. Nevertheless, they are still in danger of extinction.

Exotic pets

Reptiles have become popular pets, and the demand for rare or unusual creatures, like the spiny armadillo lizard from southern Africa, has led to a sharp decline in some populations. Up to 80 percent of caged reptiles do not survive the journeys to foreign pet stores. And, if the reptiles end up in non-expert hands, they very often become ill and die.

The ecological balance of the habitat these reptiles leave behind is also damaged. If too many snakes are taken from an area, the remaining mouse or rat population grows out of control. Reptiles are wild animals that need their natural habitats as much as their natural habitats need them.

When threatened, the armadillo lizard rolls itself up into a ball, gripping its tail firmly in its mouth. This pose protects its soft belly and presents an unappetizing spiky ring to a hungry eagle. However, it won't save the lizard from capture by someone hoping to sell it as part of the illegal pet trade.

Mysterious reptiles

The ajolote, or Mexican worm-lizard, is one of the strangest-looking reptiles of all. It is not actually a lizard and it's not a snake either. It's an amphisbaenian and is related to snakes and lizards, such as geckos and skinks. The worm-lizard has forelimbs at the front of its long, pink, ringed body, but no hind limbs. It lives underground, so we do not know much about its life. Although reptiles should not be kept as pets, it is important that scientists are able to study them so that we can understand and protect them and their environments.

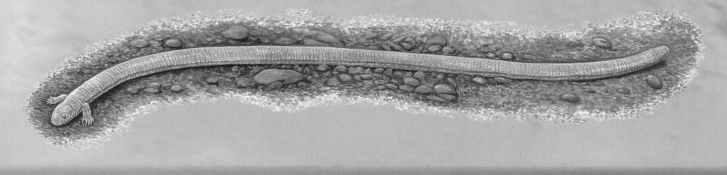

Hawksbill turtle

Vulnerable babies

Once the eggs are laid, the turtles' problems are not over. The tiny hatchlings have to dig themselves out of their sandy nest and then face a perilous dash across the beach to the ocean. Pulling themselves awkwardly over the sand with their tiny flippers, the hatchlings are helpless if preyed upon by crabs, gulls, or lizards.

The female hawksbill turtle digs a deep burrow with her back flippers. After laying up to 200 eggs, she covers them with sand and returns to the ocean. After about two months, the tiny hatchlings emerge and head for the sea. They are probably guided by the reflection of the moon and stars on the water's surface. Lights from buildings near the shore can confuse the turtles, preventing them from reaching the ocean.

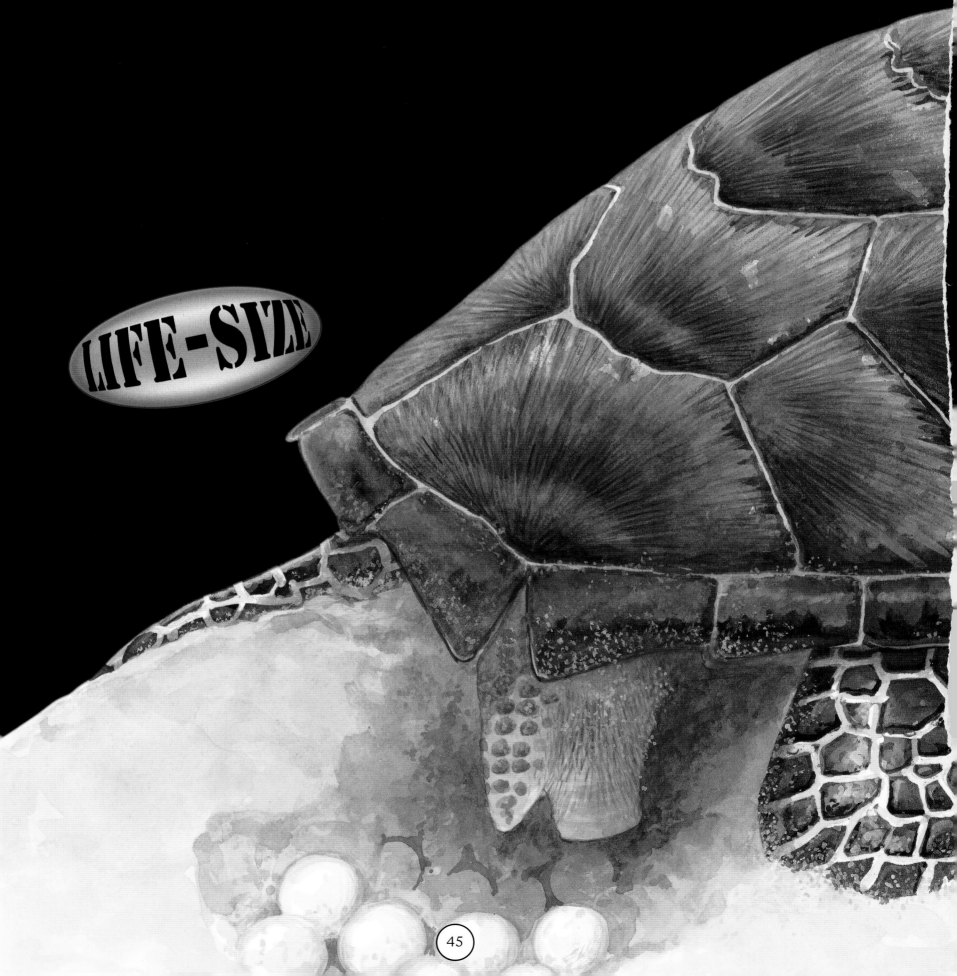

All sea turtles are endangered. They are hunted for food and for their shells, which are used to make jewelry. Female sea turtles must also take a risk when coming ashore to lay eggs. They prefer to make their nests on long, sandy beaches, but that is also where humans like to spend their holidays. Too many people on a beach will scare the turtles away, and many can't find a place for their eggs.

LIFE-SIZE

INDEX